MIX
Papier aus verantwortungsvollen Quellen
Paper from responsible sources
FSC® C105338

Franz Gosch

Solutions to master the Demographic Change

Ambient Assisted Living for the Elderly

Anchor Compact

Gosch, Franz: Solutions to master the Demographic Change: Ambient Assisted Living for the Elderly. Hamburg, Anchor Academic Publishing 2013
Original title of the thesis: Ambient Assisted Living for the Elderly

Buch-ISBN: 978-3-95489-111-5
PDF-eBook-ISBN: 978-3-95489-611-0
Druck/Herstellung: Anchor Academic Publishing, Hamburg, 2013
Additionally: Niederlande, Maastricht University, Bachelor Thesis, 2012.

Bibliografische Information der Deutschen Nationalbibliothek:
Die Deutsche Nationalbibliothek verzeichnet diese Publikation in der Deutschen Nationalbibliografie; detaillierte bibliografische Daten sind im Internet über http://dnb.d-nb.de abrufbar

Bibliographical Information of the German National Library:
The German National Library lists this publication in the German National Bibliography. Detailed bibliographic data can be found at: http://dnb.d-nb.de

All rights reserved. This publication may not be reproduced, stored in a retrieval system or transmitted, in any form or by any means, electronic, mechanical, photocopying, recording or otherwise, without the prior permission of the publishers.

Das Werk einschließlich aller seiner Teile ist urheberrechtlich geschützt. Jede Verwertung außerhalb der Grenzen des Urheberrechtsgesetzes ist ohne Zustimmung des Verlages unzulässig und strafbar. Dies gilt insbesondere für Vervielfältigungen, Übersetzungen, Mikroverfilmungen und die Einspeicherung und Bearbeitung in elektronischen Systemen.

Die Wiedergabe von Gebrauchsnamen, Handelsnamen, Warenbezeichnungen usw. in diesem Werk berechtigt auch ohne besondere Kennzeichnung nicht zu der Annahme, dass solche Namen im Sinne der Warenzeichen- und Markenschutz-Gesetzgebung als frei zu betrachten wären und daher von jedermann benutzt werden dürften.

Die Informationen in diesem Werk wurden mit Sorgfalt erarbeitet. Dennoch können Fehler nicht vollständig ausgeschlossen werden und die Diplomica Verlag GmbH, die Autoren oder Übersetzer übernehmen keine juristische Verantwortung oder irgendeine Haftung für evtl. verbliebene fehlerhafte Angaben und deren Folgen.

Alle Rechte vorbehalten

© Anchor Academic Publishing, ein Imprint der Diplomica® Verlag GmbH
http://www.diplom.de, Hamburg 2013
Printed in Germany

Table of contents

1. **Introduction** 7
   1.1 Background 7
   1.2 Central research question and research objectives 9
   1.3 Methodological approach and structure of the study 10
2. **Theoretical framework** 11
   2.1 Diffusion of Innovations Theory 11
   2.2 The application of the Diffusion of Innovations Theory 13
3. **Methodology** 15
   3.1 Nature of the research 15
   3.2 Steps in the research procedure 15
   3.3 Review of EU policies, projects, and initiatives 15
   3.4 Review of studies on AAL 16
   3.5 Reliability and validity 17
4. **Results** 19
   4.1 EU actions towards AAL (results of document analysis) 19
   4.2 Ambient Assisted Living at a glance
       (results of systematic literature review) 25
   4.3 Main results 32
5. **Discussion** 37
   5.1 Discussion of AAL on grounds of the Diffusion of Innovations Theory 37
   5.2 Discussion of methods 38
   5.3 Answer to the research question 40
   5.4 Recommendations and conclusion 41

List of abbreviations

AAL – Ambient Assisted Living

EU – European Union

ICT – Information and Communication Technologies

DoI – Diffusion of Innovations theory

FP6 – Sixth framework programme

AAL Joint Programme – Ambient Assisted Living Joint Programme

FP7 – Seventh framework programme

ADL – Activities of Daily Living

MS – (EU) Member States

List of figures, boxes and tables

Figure 1: Population structure by major age groups, EU-27, 1990-2060

Figure 2: Research framework

Box 1: Background and potential of ICT-enabled solutions for the elderly

Table 1: Categorization scheme of AAL domains

Table 2: Categorization of challenges of AAL

Table 3: EU actions towards AAL

Table 4: AAL at a glance

Table 5: Challenges of AAL

1 Introduction

1.1 Background

Today's modern society is characterized by its vast and rapid changes in most facets of human and environmental life. Through globalization, challenges that where faced by single countries in the past, today concern groups of countries as a whole as for instance the demographic changes that will reinvent our future. On the one hand, improvements in public health such as sanitation and food hygiene, as well as new medical technologies and solutions have altered and expanded the lifespan that humans are expected to live. On the other hand, through the industrial revolution, the trend to urbanization, and improvement in levels of education, the priorities of people have changed throughout the last generations and so have values and norms that shape contemporary societies (Lee & Reher, 2011). Today, people place more value on their careers and life attainment than ever before and delay family planning decisions through means of contraception, resulting in very low fertility rates. Reasons for this decline have been researched tremendously, but a single reason could not be identified. Rather, the decline is the consequence of changes in social life and economic circumstances throughout the past generations (Lutz, 2006).

After the baby boom in the 1960s, fertility rates have been declining for decades (Eurostat, 2012a). Simultaneously, the gaps between European countries concerning fertility rates have been converging and the latest 2009 Eurostat data for the whole European Union (EU) identifies only one single country (Ireland) that still meets the replacement level, which is considered to be 2.1 children per woman (2012). While in 2002 fertility rates of only 1.45 births have been observed in the EU-27, this has slightly improved to an average of 1.59 in 2009, although some countries still face extremely low rates, such as Germany (1.36), Portugal (1.32) or Latvia (1.31) (Eurostat, 2012b). The trend of decreasing fertility rates has been accompanied by a declining mortality, due to investments in health care and improvements in health awareness among people in developed countries (Grundy, Tomassini, & Festy, 2006). According to Eurostat statistics, the proportion of elderly people in Europe is increasing immensely. While the proportion of the European population aged 65 and older was 17.4 in 2010, it is projected to be 20.6 in 2020 and even 23.6 in 2030 (see Figure 1), implying that almost a quarter of European citizens will be 65 and older in 2030 (Eurostat, 2011). Hence, while fewer children are born, death is prolonged and people become older. This scenario of demographic changes in the western world raises questions to which answers are rather unclear, as for instance: Who will care for the elderly and how will this look like?

Figure 1: Population structure by major age groups, EU-27, 1990-2060. From: Population structure and ageing, by Eurostat, 2011. Adapted with permission.

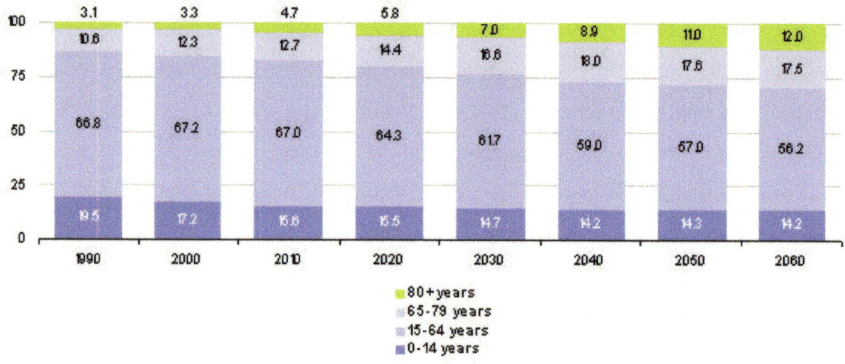

Although in some European countries family networks still act as care-giving networks for elderly relatives, this constellation is vanishing slowly and is being replaced by more narrow families with children living far away from their parents. This is reflected by a significant decline in multigenerational households over the past 30 years, although regional differences remain (Grundy, et al., 2006). Hence, through weakening family bonds, access to family care for elderly persons declines while at the same time the demand is on the rise. Other options for elderly persons who are in need of care or assistance are available, too, as for instance nursing homes.

However, according to the Eurobarometer 283, the vast majority (78%) of the European elderly population aged 55 and older prefers to be cared for at home, either by a relative or by a professional. Moreover, nursing homes are rated as being not affordable or hardly affordable by the majority (45%) of persons with an elderly parent living in such an institution (European Commission, 2007). Hence, the question arises, how future care for the elderly will look like in times when children drop out of the care-giving chain. The answer to this question may be ambient assisted living (AAL), a branch of information and communication technologies (ICT) aiming at keeping elderly persons as independent as possible in their familiar surroundings in order to postpone hospitalization. AAL can be defined as: 'aiming to prolong the time people can live in a decent way in their own home by increasing their autonomy and self-confidence, the discharge of activities of daily living, to monitor and care for the elderly or ill person, to enhance the security and to save resources' (Jara, Zamora, & Skarmeta, 2009). Moreover, AAL solutions have the potential to improve quality of life (physical, mental, social) of elder persons (Belbachir, Drobics, & Marschitz, 2010). Examples of AAL solutions are for instance sensors that detect a person falling, immediately submitting an emergency signal according to the intensity of the fall (Srp & Vajda, 2010), or computerized screen technologies directly giving suggestions for meals according to the individual diet or even ordering food (Ruyter, Zwartkruis-Pelgrim, & Aarts, 2010). Hence, with AAL solutions, people can remain independent for a longer period of time by postponing the need for human interaction (Belbachir, et al., 2010). Another social aspect is that AAL solutions can contribute to social interaction of the users, since they are kept in the familiar surroundings (Belbachir, et al., 2010; Moumtzi, Wills, & Koumpis, 2010; O'Grady, Muldoon, Dragone, Tynan, & O'Hare, 2010).

The EU plays a major role in developing AAL solutions and enhancing research in the area of ICT, as depicted by the 6th framework programme 2002-2006 or the EU's e-inclusion policy featuring the Digital Agenda 2010, just to name examples (European Commission, 2002; 2007; 2010). However, it remains questionable which challenges AAL – seen as an innovation – faces.

1.2 Central research question and research objectives

The aim of the research in this study is to present the field of AAL with relation to home care. Furthermore, the work of the European Union (EU) in the field of AAL is presented, as the EU is a major key player in enhancing research on AAL solutions that help meeting the demands of the future. Moreover, a categorization scheme of AAL solutions is developed through research evidence. Eventually, knowledge and evidence from the research conducted is used to give recommendations for the future concerning the diffusion of AAL and research directions.

Central research question the research seeks to answer:

- What is the EU-added value of AAL to elderly care and what are the challenges for diffusion of these innovative technologies?

Research objectives:

- A short elaboration about the demographic transition, with facts and figures and projections for the future with a focus on the elderly generation (introductory section)

- Data collection and analysis of relevant EU actions
- Data collection of relevant articles on AAL; discussion of those based on the Diffusion of Innovations theory in order to identify challenges
- Framing of recommendations on how to deal with AAL in order to meet the challenges of the future

1.3 Methodological approach and structure of the study

In order to answer the research question and the objectives, the study first presents the theoretical framework that is used for the research, i.e. the Diffusion of Innovations Theory. Thereafter, a chapter on the methodology follows, which is characterized by a dual nature, as it involves a document analysis and a systematic literature review. Subsequently, the paper presents the results of the research, divided into EU actions and initiatives and ambient assisted living at a glance with categorizations of its types and related challenges. Finally, the last chapter discusses the findings, answers the research question and gives recommendations on how the diffusion of AAL can be enhanced.

2 Theoretical framework

2.1 Diffusion of Innovations Theory

The theory that is used for the analysis is the 'Diffusion of Innovations theory' (DoI). Although it has been discussed by French sociologists in the early 20th century already, the American Everett M. Rogers further developed the theory to what it is today. In very general terms, it describes the process by which an innovation, which can be a product, a way of thinking, or the like, comes into the social system, hence into use. In 1962, Rogers published the first edition of this book 'Diffusion of Innovations' in which he elaborates on the theory. The most current version of his theory is presented in the fifth edition of 'Diffusion of Innovation' (2003). For the development of the theory, he gathered research evidence from over 500 studies dealing with the diffusion and adoption of innovations. According to Robinson (2009), the insights that Rogers' theory provides are verified by over 6000 field tests and studies and are therefore considered as highly reliable. The central issues of the theory focus on the process of social change and seek to present how an innovation is taken up among members of a specific population. In his book, Rogers concentrates on four main elements with regard to the diffusion of an innovation. These are the innovation itself, communication channels, time, and social system. The next paragraphs review the different dimensions of the theory, based on the works of Clarke, Kaminski, Orr, Robinson, Rogers, and Rogers and Scott (1999; 2011; 2003; 2009; 2003, 1997).

With regard to the innovation, Rogers identified certain characteristics that determine whether an innovation will be successful in its adoption. The ultimate end of a diffusion process is called saturation point, i.e. the moment when the innovation is fully integrated. The first characteristic is **relative advantage** and describes in which way it is better than current practice. However, there are no specific attributes that constitute 'relative advantage'. Therefore it is depending on wishes, needs, and perceptions of the users. The greater the perception of this characteristic, the faster is the innovation likely to be adopted. The second characteristic is **compatibility** concerning the consistency with socio-cultural values, specific needs, and practices. If an innovation is not compatible with norms and values of the target group, its adoption process is considerably slowed down. The third characteristic, **complexity**, refers to the nature of the innovation and the question whether it is simple to use or not. Simple ideas that are easy to understand have a more rapid adoption process than ideas that are more difficult. In the latter case, users that are to adopt the innovation may have to build up new ways of thinking or skills in order to understand the innovation, which slows down the adoption process, too. **Trialability** presents the fourth characteristic discussed by Rogers and concerns the possibility whether it is possible to try the innovation or not. Given the case that it is not possible to try out the innovation, high levels of uncertainty may arise. As uncertainty presents a severe obstacle in the adoption process, an innovation should ideally be trialable. The last characteristic identified by Rogers is **observability** and refers to whether positive results are visible. The more positive results are easily visible to people, the lower is the rate of uncertainty associated with the innovation. Moreover, visibility of positive results also encourages people to talk about it. Another key principle that can be linked to the successfulness of an innovation is the consideration of **re-invention**, yet it is not specifically included as a characteristic for a successful innovation. Accordingly, an innovation is even more likely to reach the saturation point, if it is possible to alter and amend the innovation during the implementation phase, according to changing needs or as challenges emerge. The notion of re-invention is essential because it refers to continuous improvements of the innovation, which are important for its successful diffusion.

With regard to communication channels, Roger identified two types of channels through which an innovation is communicated, i.e. the mass media and interpersonal channels. Mass media has the advantage that it spreads information rapidly and to many people at once. Hence, the mass media channel is essential for raising awareness about the innovation itself. However, the effect of interpersonal channels is immense, too, as strong attitudes are formed when people communicate with each other (Orr, 2003). Therefore, this channel is essential for the influence on decisions of people whether to adopt or reject the innovation. These two channels ultimately influence the pace and the quality of the adoption process.

The dimension of time in the theory focuses on three ways of time involvement. The first way is the innovation-decision process, which can be looked upon in five steps. These steps encompass: ***knowledge***, referring to knowing what it is about and recognizing the function of the innovation; ***persuasion***, in terms of realizing that it is beneficial; ***decision***, referring to deciding about its introduction; ***implementation***; and ***confirmation***, in terms of whether it yields beneficial results. As already noted, the ultimate end of an innovation is when it reached its saturation point. The second way of time involvement is the degree of innovativeness of people of the social system and refers to the specific types of people that are involved in the adoption process as time passes by. The theory categorizes and characterizes these groups of people. These include: innovators, early adopters, early majority, late majority, and laggards. However, a detailed characterization of each of the groups is not necessarily relevant, yet it has to be stressed that the first two groups are especially necessary. The innovators present a small group of idealistic people, which put great creativity and energy into the development of new ideas and innovations and without those people, there would not be any innovation. Soon after the innovators made the benefits of the idea or innovation visible, early adopters become aware of it and start involving in the process either in a purely private way or in seeking business opportunities. Whereas innovators and early adopters present the smallest segments of a social system, the other three groups present the bigger segments and adopt the idea or innovation one after another. The third way of time involvement refers to the rate of adoption. This rate is influenced by the successfulness of the innovation, characterized through the characteristics presented earlier and presents the pace of diffusion, usually measured in how many people of the social system adopt it in a specific period of time.

The fourth element that Rogers describes in his theory is the social system. Accordingly, a social system is defined as 'a set of interrelated units that are engaged in joint problem solving to accomplish a common goal' (Rogers, 2003). Members of a system are not necessarily specified, therefore units of a social system can be comprised of organizations, individuals, or other groups of people that have something in common or share common views.

2.2 The application of the Diffusion of Innovations theory

In the context of this study, the Diffusion of Innovations theory serves as a framework to discuss AAL solutions and technologies in light of care for the elderly (see Figure 2). The five characteristics that have been identified to constitute a successful intervention are the main focus when the theory is applied on AAL. Moreover, the consideration of re-invention is considered a characteristic of a successful innovation, too, and is therefore included in the analysis as a characteristic. Hence, the discussion of AAL will follow the characteristics of observability, relative advantage, compatability, trialability, complexity, and re-invention, which have already been depicted in the previous section. An elaboration on each of these characteristics emphasizes the potential challenges of AAL solutions while also revealing challenges and barriers for diffusion. The analysis only focuses on these characteristics and does not go beyond them or considers other dimensions of the theory, as the scope of this study is not be exceeded.

Figure 2: Research framework

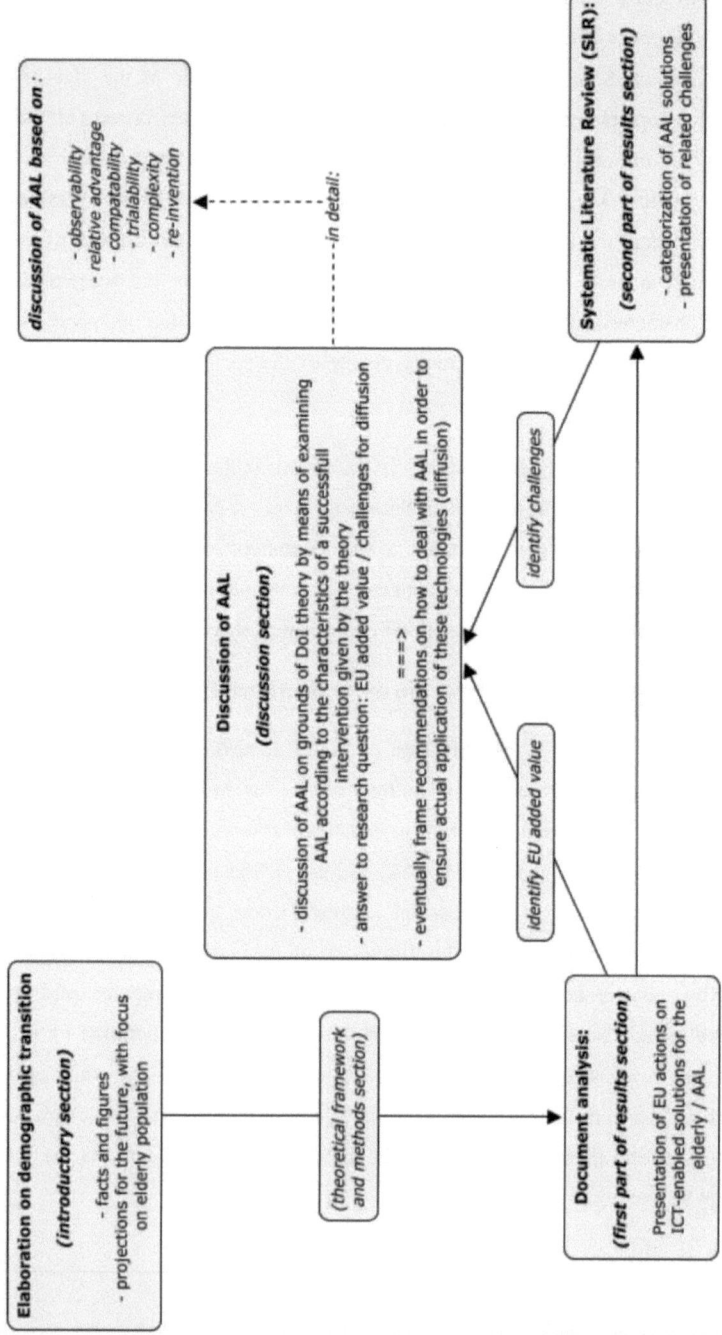

3 Methodology

3.1 Nature of the research

The research focuses on a review of secondary sources, including a review of EU actions towards AAL and a review of research evidence on AAL published in peer-reviewed journals; hence it is a secondary research (desk research) on already existing publications. The character of the study is both explorative and explanatory as it dives into the topic of AAL solutions for the elderly while also revealing related challenges. The part on EU actions is based on a document analysis, while the part on research evidence on AAL is based on a systematic literature review.

3.2 Steps in the research procedure

In general terms, the secondary research encompasses the following steps.

Step I – gathering information on relevant EU policies, projects, and initiatives
Step II – gathering information on AAL

    II.1- Identifying sources of information

    II.2- Gathering existing data

    II.3- Normalizing data (in terms of identifying aspects that can be compared in a qualitative or even quantitative way)

    II.4- Analyzing the data

These steps are based on a workbook on secondary research, provided by Market Street Research (MSR), which is a marketing research company also in the field of healthcare market research (MSR, n.d.).

3.3 Review of EU policies, projects, and initiatives

Sources of information for the EU related aspects are official websites of the EU, such as https://ec.europa.eu. This part only focuses on official EU publications (strategy documents, communications, decisions, etc.) directly obtained via websites of the EU, such as the official website of the European Commission (ec.europa.eu) or the official website of the European Statistical Office (https://epp.eurostat.ec.europa.eu) in order to ensure coherence and scientific validity. This aims to ensure the identification of the pure EU added value. Furthermore, only information and data available in English language is used with a focus on documents issued between 2005 and 2012. Search terms that were used are: 'ambient assisted living' and 'AAL' with amendments to 'European Union' and 'EU'. As the step of normalizing data does not apply to a document analysis, it is excluded. The presentation of the results focuses on the research question in order to ensure that the scope of the study is not exceeded. Hence, the presentation of the results of EU-related matters aims to determine whether there is an EU-added value of AAL to the field of elderly care, which is discussed in the discussion section.

3.4 Review of studies on AAL

Sources of information for the systematic literature review on AAL are the following online databases:

- Oxford Journals,
- PubMed,
- ScienceDirect (Elsevier),
- SpringerLink and
- Web of Science.

Keywords for the data gathering are: 'ambient assisted living', 'ambient assisted living challenges', as well as amendments to 'AAL' instead of 'ambient assisted living'. In order to limit the scope of the systematic literature review, certain limitation criteria are applied. The part on AAL solutions and technologies is limited to European publications. Additionally, it only includes publications from 2005 onwards and only those in English language. Moreover, book sections are excluded; therefore the focus lies on journal articles. An article is considered relevant when it not only focuses on technological issues but also discusses AAL solutions from other perspectives, as for instance the user perspective or a public health perspective. In the case of this qualitative research, normalizing data is a process within data analysis and deals with categorizing and coding of data that has been gathered. The analysis of the received documents deals with categorizing the discussed solutions in different domains in a mutually exclusive way and stating the frequencies of its emergence. Furthermore, challenges mentioned in the articles are written down, grouped, and mentioned together with the respective frequencies.

In detail, the analysis of the data gathered involves specific steps based on Pope, Ziebland & Mays (2000). Firstly, all literature needs to be read by the researcher in order to identify common themes and obtain a rough overview. Moreover, literature that came up during the data gathering process which is absolutely not related to the research objectives can already be excluded. Secondly, themes within the literature that are related to the different research objectives need to be identified. This process usually involves coding of text-phrases. For the sake of accuracy, each research objective obtains an overall category. Thereafter, all text phrases, themes, common concepts and the like are ordered in order to obtain information for each category separately. The next step involves looking at the data for each category (i.e. constant comparison) and coding common themes, concepts and the like. Through this process, the frequency of each coded item (how many times it emerged in the literature) can be recorded in order to judge its importance and validity. Usually it is desired that the categories as well as the coded items are mutually exclusive. The analytical writing process focuses on the coded items, their frequency and importance for each category.

3.5 Reliability and validity

In qualitative research, notions of reliability and validity are manifold and sometimes even contradictory. Some researchers, as for instance Golafshani, argue that in qualitative research, reliability is not more than purely the consequence of validity (2003). However, this research makes a difference between reliability and validity, based on the work of Lawrence Neuman (2006). Accordingly, qualitative reliability refers to the consistency in the use of methods to oberserve and capture the desired context in a unique research setting. In this particular research setting, reliability with regard to the document analysis is ensured by the use of official EU publications received through the website of the European Commission. With regard to the systematic literature review on AAL, the use of different scientific databases with a limitation to certain criteria and settings ensures reliability. Hence, for both the document analysis and the systematic literature review, consistency of methods is ensured.

With regard to validity, Neuman puts emphasis on concepts such as authenticity and truthfulness, referring to whether the studied context is true and credible (2006). The term generalizability does not necessarily apply to qualitative research, as research evidence from a particular research setting focuses on a specific geographical context or a given period in time, and does therefore not allow generalizing research findings from one specific and unique setting to other settings. Hence, the question remains how to ensure validity in this research. With regard to the document analysis, it is assumed that the received documents have a high degree of validity as they are issued by official organs of the European Union. With regard to the systematic literature review, mostly peer-reviewed journal articles are used, which already have a high degree of validity, too. However, an additional method to further ensure validity for the results of the systematic literature review is that of triangulation. The core idea of triangulation is to gather findings from independent sources in order to see whether they yield consistent findings (Neumann, 2006). Hence, with regard to the systematic literature review, the method of triangulation confirms the findings when for instance a specific challenge of AAL systems is mentioned by various authors. In order to indicate triangulation with regard to the results of this research, frequencies of emergence of certain aspects are noted down and added to the tables of the results section.

4 Results

4.1 EU actions towards AAL (results of document analysis)

The next paragraphs present the work of the EU in the field of ICT-enabled solutions targeted at the elderly population throughout the past seven years. In total, 22 documents were used for this section. Except for two documents of the Ambient Assisted Joint Programme initiated by the EU, all documents were issued by European Institutions, mostly the European Commission. As the search term 'ambient assisted living' on the website of the European Commission yields hundreds of matches including press releases and archived news, this section presents the most important actions of the EU in the light of AAL. With the aid of the 22 documents, the progress of the EU in terms of AAL is made visible. However, especially at the beginning of the time span, the term AAL had not established itself. Therefore, also actions that directly link ICT-enabled solutions with the elderly population are presented, as this is what AAL emerged from.

Sixth framework programme (FP6)

Since 1984, the EU launches multiannual framework programmes aimed at boosting research and technological developments and promote growth through financial and political instruments. The 'Sixth Framework Programme of the European Community for research, technological development and demonstration activities' from 2002 to 2006 does not mention specific actions in the field of elderly care, demographics or AAL, yet it has to be considered an action towards AAL (European Commission, 2002). This is because large amounts of money have been allocated to boost research in the area of ICT, which in these past days have been regarded as 'Information Society Technologies'. According to the Commission of the European Communities (2002), the main objective of the theme 'information society technologies' within the framework programme is to develop technologies that are user-friendly and among other focus groups, the elderly population is mentioned as a target group, especially for 'ambient intelligence systems'.

i2010 and its consequences

In June 2005, the initiative 'i2010: European Information Society for growth and employment' was adopted by the European Commission as the first initiative after the revision of the Lisbon Strategy (European Commission, 2005). The five-year strategy was meant to support the digital economy of the EU and identified Information and Communication Technologies (ICT) as having the potential to positively contribute to personal quality of life, to society, and to economy. Three policy priority areas were therefore identified by the EU, of which one directly links to the elder society: 'To promote an inclusive European information society'. Accordingly, three ICT initiatives were meant to set up under this pillar of which one addresses 'technologies for an ageing society'. At the very end of the i2010 strategy, a Commission Staff Working Document, listing the main achievements of the strategy, was published (Commission of the European Communities, 2009a). Of the 13 action areas, Action 8 and Action 10 directly addressed the elder population. According to Action 8, a comprehensive strategy on e-inclusion was decided on throughout the course of the i2010 strategy, and so was a Ministerial Conference held in Riga in June 2006, where priorities and commitments were set to address the needs of the elder population to be included in the proposed e-inclusion strategy. Action group 10 'Ageing well in the information society' was composed of a Communication on an Action Plan concerning the use of ICT for the elderly and a proposal for participation in research and development programs aiming at improving the quality of life of the elderly by the use of ICT.

Action Plan on ageing well in the information society

The Action Plan on ageing well in the information society, issued by the Commission of the European Communities, represents a first response to the Ministerial Conference in Riga and was already announced in the course of the i2010 strategy (2007a). It again points out the importance of ICT, as it emphasizes that these technologies 'help the older individuals to improve quality of life, stay healthier and live independent for longer'. Moreover, it stresses the positive contribution that these innovative solutions can have on persons which have impaired hearing, memory, or vision. However, it also identifies that the market of such technologies for ageing well had not reached its full potential by the time the Action Plan was issued. This was due to different kinds of barriers, including mostly awareness obstacles on both the user and the industry side, and technical barriers related to user-friendliness and interoperability.

The Action Plan was the first official document illustrating the potential of ICT-enabled technologies targeted at the elderly population in short and clear terms, thereby tackling the awareness problem of the industry (see Box 1).

Box 1. Background and potential of ICT-enabled solutions for the elderly. From: *Action Plan on Ageing Well in the Information Society* (p. 7), by the Commission of the European Communities, 2007. Adapted with permission.

- Europeans over 65 possess wealth and revenues of over 3000 B€.
- The market for smart homes applications (age-related assistance in shopping, dressing, moving independently) will triple between 2005 and 2020, from 13 million people up to 37 million.
- 68 million people in 2005 had several forms of age-related impairment. This will grow to 84 million in 2020.
- Early patient discharge from hospital due to the introduction of mobile health monitoring would save €1,5 billion p.a. in Germany alone.
- EU research projects have developed technologies for personalised route guidance; home care and remote health monitoring and advice; intelligent alarms; natural interfaces for accessible ICT.

Objectives of the Action Plan are first, 'to enable a better quality of life for older people with significant cost-savings in health and social care' and second, 'to help creating a strong industrial basis in Europe for ICT and ageing'. Especially with the first objective, it aims at personalizing healthcare and social care.

Specific actions the Action Plan sought to achieve in terms of raising awareness were on the one hand the establishment of an innovation platform consisting of industry stakeholders and civil society organizations. On the other hand, the action plan announced the launch of a Ministerial Debate in late 2007 where policy proposals regarding ICT and ageing should be proposed, as well as the inclusion of ICT for ageing in the e-inclusion initiative in 2008. Additionally, the setting up of an internet portal for ICT and ageing was announced. The actual realization of these actions was not as explicit as the action plan proposed. Although the program list of the announced Ministerial Debate on e-inclusion in Lisbon mentions a low number of presentations related to ICT and ageing, those are only related to ageing at the workplace and not to ageing at home (European Commission, 2007b). Regarding the proposed innovation platform, a best-practice portal for business stakeholders has been established and can be found via www.epractice.eu. Furthermore, as announced in the Action Plan, ICT for ageing was included in the e-inclusion initiative of 2008, which this chapter deals with later on. Unfortunately, an internet portal centered on the issue of ICT for ageing has not been launched so far.

In order to overcome technical barriers, such as problems with user-friendliness of ICT enabled solutions, a major study was carried out in 2008 which analysed the usage of such products by the elderly population in order to know what future efforts should be targeted at (European Commission, 2008a).

According to the Action Plan, research and innovation needs to be boosted in order to ensure the profitable development of ICT and Ambient Assisted Living solutions targeted at elderly people. Accompanying the Action Plan was a proposal 'to support […] a new joint Europe-wide applied research programme on technologies that will help people live more comfortably in later life, called Ambient Assisted Living' (European Commission, 2007d). Hence, the Ambient Assisted Living Joint Project representing the most concrete action of the Action Plan was initiated, which the next subchapter deals with. Additionally, the Action Plan was accompanied by a press release of the European Commission, stating that from 2007 to 2013 more than €1bn will be invested into projects and programs dealing with technologies to age well (European Commission, 2007c). Of this amount, 60% will directly be invested into the Ambient Assisted Living Joint Programme.

Ambient Assisted Living Joint Programme

The Ambient Assisted Living Joint Programme represents the major keystone in the EU's work on meeting the demands of the future, imposed by the demographic change. After its preparation period from 2004 to 2006 and its first mentioning in the Action Plan for Ageing Well in the Information Society in 2007, its Commission Proposal was approved according to the co-decision procedure by the European Parliament and adopted by the European Council in 2008 (Official Journal of the European Union, 2008). It has initially been set up for the period of 2008 to 2013 and includes 23 associated states and the European Commission. Its biggest advantage is that it is a joint research programme, i.e. all national research activities of the associated countries on ICT enabled independent living for the elderly are pooled together for applied research. Moreover, all joint projects from the different countries follow one single evaluation procedure. The AAL Joint Programme is governed by the AAL Association, consisting of representatives from the associated countries and the European Commission (European Commission, 2008b). The overall objective of the programme is to 'enhance the quality of life of older people and strengthen the industrial base in Europe through the use of

Information and Communication Technologies (ICT)' (AAL Joint Programme, 2008; Official Journal of the European Union, 2008). Specific aims of the programme are as follows:

> 'To foster the emergence of innovative ICT-based products, services and systems for ageing well at home, in the community, and at work, thus improving the quality of life, autonomy, participation in social life, skills, and employability of older people and reducing the costs of health and social care'

> 'To create a critical mass of research, development and innovation at the EU level in the areas of technologies and services for ageing well in the information society [...]'

> 'To improve conditions for industrial exploitation of research results by providing a coherent European framework for developing common approaches [...]'

The main activity of the programme consists of calling for proposals for R&D projects in the field of Ambient Assisted Living at regular intervals, with specific information about the target-topic and its funding rules. If a proposal is successful, it will be funded and the respective projects can be carried out. Currently, it is the fifth call for proposals which is targeted at 'ICT-based Solutions for (Self-) Management of Daily Life Activities of Older Adults at Home' (AAL Joint Programme, 2012). At the moment of writing, 29 proposals were handed in. Very recently, on 27 April 2012, the European Parliament received several request regarding the AAL Joint Programme, dealing with the question of continuation, since the programme expires in 2013 (European Parliament, 2012). However, since it bundles more than 80 research & development & innovation projects of 23 states with end-user involvement, it is highly unlikely that the programme will stop after its expiration without any kind of continuation.

e-inclusion

The issue of e-inclusion, although it was already mentioned in 2000, emerged throughout the course of the i2010 strategy, and aims at 'enabling every person to fully participate in the information society, despite any individual or social disadvantages' (European Commission, 2007a). The Ministerial Conference in Riga in 2006 resulted in the 'Riga Declaration', signed by more than 30 countries of Europe, representing a major landmark towards an e-inclusion initiative. Under the priority area 'Address the needs of older workers and elderly people' specific targets aimed at the elderly population were set in the declaration, as for instance:

'exploiting the full potential of the internal market of ICT services and products for the elderly. [...] Barriers to innovative ICT solutions for social security and health reimbursement schemes need to be addressed, particularly at the national level.'

'Realizing increased quality of life, autonomy and safety, while respecting privacy and ethical requirements. This can be done through independent living initiatives, the promotion of assistive technologies, and ICT-enabled services for integrated social and healthcare, including personal emergency and location based services.'

As proposed for and in the i2010 strategy, a European initiative on e-inclusion was adopted in 2007 following the Riga conference (Commission of the European Communities, 2007b). The staff working document clearly identifies, that past efforts have not been enough to meet the targets of the Riga conference. Therefore the initiative on e-inclusion was adopted in order to boost progress in the field of e-inclusion by two ways: First, a campaign was launched to raise awareness for a concluding Ministerial Conference where concrete action and progress was meant to be presented. Second, the Riga Declaration was implemented into a strategic framework for action with three main objectives. Of these three, the second objective 'Accelerating effective participation of groups at risk of exclusion and improving quality of life' addresses the elderly population, as the Riga Declaration identifies elderly people, disabled people and cultural minorities as groups at risk. As specific actions to be taken regarding this objective, the Staff Working Document calls for the Commission, the industry, all single Member States and user organizations to 'implement the EU Action Plan on 'Ageing well in the information society''. Furthermore, the Commission assures to 'provide sustained support for research and for deployment on ICT-enabled innovative solutions relating to ageing, disability and health'.

Seventh framework programme (FP7)

The 'Seventh Framework Programme of the European Community for research, technological development and demonstration activities' covers the time span of 2007 to 2013 (European Commission, 2006a). Among the four main objectives of cooperation, ideas, people, and capacity, the programme of cooperation is important for the field of AAL. With regard to the cooperation programme, ICT are mentioned to be important, so that 'the changing needs of European society [...] can be met' (European Commission, 2006b). Furthermore, in close cooperation with MS, a specific initiative on ambient assisted living is to be implemented. In 2009, the Commission of the European Communities issued an official document on the progress made under the seventh framework programme (2009b). Accordingly, an initiative on AAL has been set up. However, no further specification of this statement has been given. Yet, the document also mentions that FP7 'has supported the development of novel tools and services to manage medical knowledge and deliver new ways of healthcare in particular though […] the Ambient-Assisted-Living programme and ICT for ageing well'. Moreover, a large amount of projects on AAL solutions has been funded under FP7.

Europe 2020 and the Digital Agenda

Following the i2010 strategy is the EU's new 'Europe 2020' strategy, focusing on three explicit priorities: it wants the economy of the EU to become smart, sustainable, and inclusive (2010a). However, the 35 pages document issued by the Commission deals more with how the current financial crisis can be overcome, than with specific actions targeted at the elderly population. Therefore, the terms 'elderly' or 'ambient assisted living' are not mentioned once.

Nevertheless, the Europe 2020 strategy has a link to the area of ambient assisted living for the elderly. In order to meet the priority-targets, seven flagship initiatives underpin the strategy, each addressing different themes. Among those seven is the 'Digital Agenda for Europe' which aims at high-speed internet and 'the benefits of a digital single market for households and firms'. Although the strategy document itself does not elaborate on these flagships in much detail, the European Commission communication on the Digital Agenda for Europe does (2010b). According to the action area 'ICT-enabled benefits for EU society', the take-up of solutions and technologies of independent living by the elder population shall be doubled by 2015. Furthermore, the document states the reinforcement of the AAL Joint Programme as a specific action. However, neither it is elaborated why the successful programme needs to be reinforced nor what a reinforcement will look like.

4.2 Ambient Assisted Living at a glance (results of systematic literature review)

This section deals with the documents received in the context of the systematic literature review. Although a short illustration of AAL has already been given in the introductory section, here the topic of AAL is deepened and solely based on the articles of the systematic literature review. In total, the review resulted in 32 documents. However, of those 32 documents, nine documents were received several times through the use of five databases. Additionally, one article had to be excluded due to its nature being irrelevant to the topic of ambient assisted living. Hence, an amount of 22 journal articles was used for the review. In general, all these articles had an interdisciplinary nature as none of them only dealt with a public health perspective. All 22 articles gave information regarding AAL at home, while only very few also discussed AAL in other areas, i.e. in the community and at work. Hence, this results section is focused on AAL in home environments, since this is the main topic of interest for these kinds of solutions. First, a categorization scheme of the AAL solutions discussed in the articles is presented and explained. Second, challenges that are mentioned in the articles are presented in a table view and explained, too. Instead of stating in-text citations in the paragraphs explaining the tables, this kind of information is given in the tables itself. Thereby, the reader does not become confused by great numbers of citations in the reading sections, but can refer to the tables.

Categorization of solutions

As categorizations and clear definitions in the area of AAL are either missing or contradictory, all AAL solutions from the systematic literature review were grouped according to their type. The total amount of mentioned or discussed solutions was 40. As even solutions targeted at the same purpose, as for instance at fall detection, considerably differ in their technology used, a simple categorization system had to be developed which solely concentrates on the purpose of the respective solution without demanding advanced technological knowledge. However, it is essential to know that an AAL solution is always constituted of the interplay of hardware and software. The most often used hardware components are sensors and motion capturing systems/cameras, which in 21st century open up possibilities beyond belief. These components correspond with software modules, usually situated somewhere in the near environment. Depending on the respective solution, the hard- and software either identifies certain events or supports and interacts with the user. In order to generally present the solutions from the articles, a mutually exclusive classification system had to be developed, categorizing AAL solutions into four domains. Thereby, every solution from the systematic literature review could be allocated to a domain. Table 1 presents the four areas of solutions that could be identified through the systematic literature review and is shortly explained in the coming paragraphs. The bold number in the lower right corner of the boxes indicates how often solutions with this respective purpose emerged in the articles.

The first domain of solutions are technologies monitoring housing conditions, as for instance advanced fire detection systems that go beyond simple smoke alarms. Also housing control systems which observe gas, heating and water conditions and optimize these according to best efficiency fall in this area. The second domain focuses on systems monitoring the elderly via worn or embedded sensors and camera systems in order to detect emergency situations as for instance whether an elderly has suffered a fall or recognize the activities of the elderly.

Table 1: Categorization scheme of AAL domains

Domain of solutions	Purposes within the respective group
Monitoring housing conditions *(through means of sensors)*	**Housing Control (e.g. energy use optimization)** (Belbachir, et al., 2010) n=1
	Fire detection systems (Weimar et al., 2009), (Cardinaux, Bhowmik, Abhayartne, & Hawley, 2011) n=2
	Fridge management (Picking et al., 2009) n=1
Monitoring activities of the elderly *(worn or embedded sensors, pressure pads, motion capturing systems/cameras)*	**Fall detection** (Villacorta, Val, Jimanez, & Izquierdo, 2010), (Leone, Diraco, & Siciliano, 2011), (Munoz, Augusto, Villa, & Botia, 2011), (Boulos et al., 2007), (O'Grady, et al., 2010), (Botia, Villa, & Palma, 2012), (Rodrigues, Alves, Silveira, & Laranjeira, 2012), (Belbachir, et al., 2010), (Weimar, et al., 2009), (Cardinaux, et al., 2011), (Amoretti et al., 2011), (Ayala, Amor, & Fuentes, 2012) n=12
	Person identification (Villacorta, et al., 2010) n=1
	Location identification (Boulos, et al., 2007), (O'Grady, et al., 2010) n=2
	Recognition of activities/ADL's (Chaaraoui, Climent-Pérez, & Flórez-Revuelta, 2012), (Botia, et al., 2012), (Amoretti, et al., 2011), (Ayala, et al., 2012) **Specific: support with laundry** (Picking, et al., 2009) n=5
	Identification of health problems **Specific: Hemiplegia, Parkinson's disease, pain in the back** (Pogorelc, Bosnic, & Gams, 2012), (Pogorelc et al., 2012) **Specific: Dementia** (Belbachir, et al., 2010) n=4
Monitoring biometric parameters *(via wearable devices using thermoelectric sensors)*	**Underlying technology** (Francioso et al., 2011) n=1
	Vital signs (Boulos, et al., 2007), (Rodrigues, et al., 2012), (Parente et al., 2011), (O'Grady, et al., 2010), (Cardinaux, et al., 2011), (Benghazi et al., 2012) n=6
Support disease management *(through devices such as smartphones)*	**Diabetes** (O'Grady, et al., 2010) n=1
	Medication management (Rogers, Peres, & Mueller, 2010), (Parente, et al., 2011), (Ayala, et al., 2012) n=3
	Malnutrition (Meschner et al., 2011) n=1

In the event of a fall, specific systems either interact with the elderly to check whether she or he is fine before considering a fatal event, or do directly alert emergency services. Systems designed for the recognition of activities are mainly designed to either support the user with certain activities (such as doing the laundry, giving advice what to do next) or to identify health problems. For instance Hemiplegia, a gait-related health problem, can be identified by analyzing the moving patterns of a person obtained through motion capturing systems. With regards to dementia, specific software analyses the behavior of the elderly and recognizes if certain behavior patterns change over time. The third domain is composed of systems monitoring biometric parameters of the elderly such as ECG and blood pressure. This is achieved through means of wearable devices using thermoelectric sensors. Health data of a person obtained through these systems is in most cases wirelessly transmitted to the physician and presents a main interest in telemedicine. The last domain of solutions includes those aimed at supporting the elderly with disease management, including medication management. Such solutions consist of smartphone-like devices that remind of taking medicine while also demanding from the user to confirm the intake. This is especially useful in the case of elderly persons suffering from dementia because the device compiles statistics of adherence. However, although these devices monitor the elderly, they rely on the elderly to actively use it while other monitoring systems are rather passive.

As the frequencies indicate, the area of activity monitoring received by far the most interest in recent research, especially with the domain of fall detection. The second most frequent area is the domain of monitoring vital signs of the elderly such as blood pressure and ECG. However, as this domain directly links with telemedicine it is assumed that more research has been conducted on such issues, yet not under the umbrella of ambient assisted living. In the context of solutions that aim to support the elderly with the management of chronic diseases, most research has been conducted on the issue of medication management. Monitoring of housing conditions clearly is the least frequent area of research with regard to the systematic literature review.

Challenges of AAL

In articles of the systematic literature review, a variety of challenges are mentioned with regard to AAL solutions and environments. As the multitude of authors uses different words for the same meaning, overarching categories had to be built in order to ensure a reliable presentation of challenges and requirements that AAL faces. Furthermore, for each category, a number of more specific words were added. Thereby, the reader obtains an overview, what a respective category includes. Furthermore, the presentation of the challenges and requirements is simplified in order to be understandable and comprehensible from a layman perspective. Table 2 presents the challenges which emerged in the articles and again, the bold number in the lower right corner of the boxes (n) indicates the frequency of the respective category. Furthermore, even when one article talked about more than one perspective of a challenge category, these were still counted as being mentioned once by the respective author(s). The next paragraphs explain the categories in more detail.

As the table shows, challenges of AAL are grouped into three main areas, i.e. technical challenges, challenges for the design of AAL environments, and challenges for acceptance. Technical challenges refer to very specific technological challenges and have therefore been presented as reliability challenges for the sake of simplicity. Hence, the reliability category encompasses characteristics that are vital for a reliable functioning of the solutions. This includes for instance the drawbacks of battery-driven solutions that may stop working once the battery has reached its lifespan (security) or the demand of responding and/or acting in time for example when an elderly has suffered a fall (timeliness). Moreover, false-negatives and false-positives are important parameters to consider. Thus, challenges in this area are absolutely vital for the correct functioning and therefore for safe and secure usage. They have been mentioned by twelve groups of authors.

The second category refers to challenges and requirements that arise in the context of designing AAL environments. AAL environments are composed of different single solutions that work together. As needs of elderly persons change over time, it is crucial that AAL solutions not only interact with each other, but are also designed in such a way, that other solutions can easily be integrated into the environment. Therefore, the overall challenge of 'interplay of solutions' encompasses characteristics such as extendibility, adoptability, adaptability, integrability, and simplicity. AAL solutions need to be extendable and adoptable to other solutions and these have to be easily integrated. Furthermore, they need to be adaptable in a way that they respond to the changing needs of the elderly. An amount of ten groups of authors discussed these kinds of issues in the articles. Adaptability to the user links to the second challenge in this category, i.e. proactivity. Accordingly, AAL solutions should aim at the reduction of interaction between the elderly user and the solution itself, as discussed by six groups of authors.

Table 2: Categorization of challenges of AAL

Category of challenge	Type of challenge
Technical challenges *(technical requirements in underlying solutions)*	**Reliability** - Quality - Safety - Security - Timeliness (Meschner, et al., 2011), (Benghazi, et al., 2012), (Ayala, et al., 2012), (Cardinaux, et al., 2011), (Parente, et al., 2011), (Weimar, et al., 2009), (Rodrigues, et al., 2012), (Botia, et al., 2012), (Boulos, et al., 2007), (Munoz, et al., 2011), (Leone, et al., 2011), (Francioso, et al., 2011) **n=12**
Challenges for design of AAL environments *(refers to the nature of the solutions)*	**Interplay of solutions** - Extendibility - Adoptability - Adaptability - Integrability - Simplicity (Benghazi, et al., 2012), (Ayala, et al., 2012), (Amoretti, et al., 2011), (Cardinaux, et al., 2011), (Parente, et al., 2011), (Rogers, et al., 2010), (Botia, et al., 2012), (Chaaraoui, et al., 2012), (Pogorelc, Vatavu, et al., 2012), (Picking, et al., 2009) **n=10**
	Proactivity - Reduction of interaction between elderly and solution (Ayala, et al., 2012), (Cardinaux, et al., 2011), (Weimar, et al., 2009), (Botia, et al., 2012), (O'Grady, et al., 2010), (Picking, et al., 2009) **n=6**
	Lack of user integration (in development) - Acknowledgement of heterogeneity of the elderly - Identification of wishes - Identification of needs (Meschner, et al., 2011), (Ayala, et al., 2012), (Weimar, et al., 2009), (Belbachir, et al., 2010), (O'Grady, et al., 2010), (Pogorelc, Vatavu, et al., 2012) **n=6**
Challenges for acceptance *(from the user perspective)*	**User perception** - Data protection - Privacy (Meschner, et al., 2011), (Cardinaux, et al., 2011), (Belbachir, et al., 2010), (Boulos, et al., 2007), (Picking, et al., 2009), (Pogorelc, Bosnic, et al., 2012), (Leone, et al., 2011), (Francioso, et al., 2011) **n=8**
	Social disconnectivity (Cardinaux, et al., 2011), (Botia, et al., 2012), (Pogorelc, Vatavu, et al., 2012), (Picking, et al., 2009) **n=4**
	Specific characteristics of target population - Low technological knowledge (Ayala, et al., 2012), (Cardinaux, et al., 2011) **n=2**

Hence, although interactivity is an important issue with regard to the solutions, it is not aimed for in the context of the user, as solutions should work automatically without demanding too much action from the user. A third challenge in the category of challenges for design of AAL environments is the lack of user involvement in the development process. Accordingly, the heterogeneity of the elderly population is not acknowledged by many AAL solutions, and therefore specific needs are not addressed appropriately. Hence, six groups of authors emphasize the importance of user involvement in order to address specific needs and whishes from the beginning on.

The third category refers to challenges that may hamper the acceptance from sides of the elderly. The most prominent challenge in this regard is the user perception of data protection and privacy. As discussed by eight groups of authors, elderly persons may feel the risk of loss of privacy, especially when they are involved in activity monitoring systems or motion capturing systems. Furthermore, the feeling that data of oneself is not safe is an important issue to consider. However, concerns of data protection may be decreased, when certain methods to ensure confidential use of data are applied. Nevertheless, loss of privacy cannot be eliminated. Therefore, the right level between an efficient working of the system and loss of privacy has to be found. Social disconnectivity has been discussed by four articles and relates to the perception, that through AAL solutions, elderly people lose social bonds, as they only interact with electronic means instead of a human caregiver. The last area of the third category of challenges refers to a specific characteristic of the target population, i.e. a low level of technological knowledge. This induces skepticism among the elderly of today towards AAL solutions and environments and is an important issue to consider for the diffusion of AAL.

4.3 Main results

This section presents both the results of EU actions towards AAL and the results of the systematic literature review in table views (for a summary see table 3, 4, and 5). Additionally, a short explaining paragraph is added for each table.

With regard to the EU actions (table 3), progress from sides of the EU has been made visible by the document analysis. Through the sixth framework programme emphasis has been laid on ICT products that are targeted at the elderly population. The i2010 initiative has made further steps as the development of the e-inclusion strategy was decided on in the context of the Ministerial Conference in Riga. Furthermore, it was decided to develop an action plan on ageing well in the information society. This action plan, issued in 2007, identified technical and awareness barriers for the diffusion of ICT-enabled solutions for the elderly and illustrated the full potential of those in short and clear terms.

Table 3: EU actions towards AAL

Field of Actions	Characteristics, actions
Sixth framework programme (2002-2006)	- Develop user-friendly ICT targeted at the elderly population - Focus on 'ambient intelligence systems'
i2010 initiative (2005-2010)	- Action 8: develop e-inclusion initiative o Riga Conference on e-inclusion - Action 10: Develop action plan on ageing well in the information society

Action Plan on ageing well in the information society (2007)	- Identified barriers for diffusion of AAL: awareness, technical barriers
	- Illustrates the potential of ICT-enabled technologies in short and clear terms
	- Actions:
	   o Ministerial debate with presentations of ICT linked with ageing
	   o Establishment of best-practice portal (internet)
	   o Again announced inclusion of ICT for ageing in e-inclusion initiative
	   o Initiation of Ambient Assisted Living Joint Programme

Ambient Assisted Living Joint Programme (2008-2013)	- Major keystone in EU's work on meeting the demands of the demographic change, 23 associated countries + EC - Biggest advantage: joint research programme, i.e. all national AAL activities are pooled together for applied research - Calls for proposals for R&D projects regarding AAL at regular intervals - All joint projects follow one single evaluation procedure - Currently: 29 proposals for fifth call, 'ICT-based Solutions for (Self-) Management of Daily Life Activities of Older Adults at Home'

e-inclusion initiative (2007)	- Creation of Riga Declaration
	- With regard to AAL, boost progress in two ways:
	   o Launch of a campaign to raise awareness and carry out Ministerial Conference
	   o Implement Riga Declaration
	- Furthermore, MS shall implement Action Plan on Ageing well
	- Commission assures to provide support for R&D

Seventh framework programme (2007-2013)	- Set up initiative on AAL - Developed novel tools and services through the AAL programme - Allocated large amount of money in order to fund AAL projects
Europe 2020 / Digital Agenda (2010)	- Double take-up of solutions and technologies of independent living by 2015 - Reinforce AAL Joint Programme

Specific actions that arose through the action plan were a ministerial debate with presentations on the linkage between ICT and ageing, the establishment of a best-practice portal in the internet, and the repeated announcement of the inclusion of ICT for ageing in the e-inclusion initiative. Moreover, the most important keystone for AAL has been initiated: The Ambient Assisted Living Joint Programme. This transnational joint research programme pools all national activities on AAL together for applied research. Moreover, in yearly intervals the joint programme calls for proposals for R&D projects on specific issues related to AAL. At the moment, this is 'ICT-based Solutions for (Self-) Management of Daily Life Activities of Older Adults at Home'. With regard to the e-inclusion initiative and AAL, the EU launched a campaign to raise awareness. Furthermore, the Riga Declaration was implemented into a strategic framework, also addressing the elderly, as they were identified as a risk of exclusion group. Moreover, the Commission called for MS and the industry to implement the action plan on ageing well. Following the e-inclusion initiative was the seventh framework program, which mainly allocated large amounts of money in order to fund AAL projects. Within the Europe 2020 strategy, the Digital Agenda aims at doubling the take up of solutions and technologies aimed at independent living by 2015 and at the reinforcement of the AAL programme.

With regard to the systematic literature review (table 4), a categorization scheme was developed which classified the AAL solutions from the articles into different categories and presented frequencies of emersion in the review. The four categories that were set up are: Monitoring housing conditions, monitoring activities of the elderly, monitoring biometric parameters, supportive in disease management. The first category promotes secure environments for the elderly by monitoring housing conditions and emerged four times. The second category 'Monitoring activities of the elderly' aims at the identification of fatal events and health problems with a clear predominance on fall detection. However, activity monitoring receives much focus, too. With regard to 'Monitoring biometric parameters', constant monitoring of health data is enabled; these kind of solutions emerged seven times. The last domain, 'Supportive in disease management' supports the elderly with the management of chronic diseases or health conditions, as for instance diabetes and malnutrition. A clear direction towards medication management was visible with regard to this domain.

Table 4: AAL at a glance

Domain of solution	Short presentation of characteristics and frequencies of emersion
Monitoring housing conditions	- Promotes secure environments for the elderly, also focus on energy consumption - Emerged four times - no direction of research identifiable
Monitoring activities of the elderly	- Enables the identification of fatal events of the elderly, also focus on identification of health problems - Emerged 24 times - Domain of fall detection clearly most prevalent (twelve times) - Activity monitoring receives much focus, too
Monitoring biometric parameters	- Enables constant monitoring of health data for the physicians of elderly persons - Emerged seven times - Nothing new, therefore recent research has not been extensive in the field of AAL
Supportive in disease management	- Supports the elderly with the management of chronic diseases - Emerged five times - Clear direction towards medication management (three times)

Challenges of AAL (table 5) that were mentioned in the articles of the systematic literature review were grouped in three general categories of challenges: technical challenges, challenges for the design of AAL environments, and challenges for acceptance. For each category, more specific challenges were added. In the context of technical challenges, reliability is the main challenge for AAL solutions, encompassing concepts such as quality, safety, and timeliness.

Table 5: Challenges of AAL

Category of challenge	Type of challenge
Technical challenges	Reliability (mentioned in twelve articles)
Challenges for design of AAL environments	Interplay of solutions (ten articles) Proactivity (six articles) User integration (six articles)
Challenges for acceptance	User perception of privacy and data protection (eight articles) Social disconnectivity (four articles) Characteristics of target population (two articles)

Reliability challenges were mentioned twelve times. With regard to challenges for the design of AAL environments, interplay of solutions, proactivity and user integration are important things to consider. Interplay of solutions refers to abilities of the solutions, such as extendibility and integrability and was mentioned in ten articles. Proactivity refers to the reduction of interplay between human and technique and was mentioned in six articles. The last challenge in the second category is user integration in order to identify specific needs and wishes of the target group and was discussed in six articles, too. The third category of challenges, challenges for acceptance, includes the user perception of privacy and data protection issues, which was mentioned in eight articles. Furthermore, social disconnectivity of an elderly, induced through the substitution of human caregivers through technology was discussed in four articles. The last challenge in the third category is the low technological knowledge of the elderly, which may further challenge acceptance and was discussed two times.

5 Discussion

5.1 Discussion of AAL on grounds of the Diffusion of Innovations Theory

The next paragraphs discuss whether AAL – seen as one innovation – can be seen as a successful innovation based on characteristics given by the theory. According to the theory, an innovation does not necessarily need to be a single product; also a way of thinking or an idea can be seen as an innovation.

With regard to **observability**, referring to whether positive results are visible, it can be stated that AAL meets this characteristic in a sufficient way. However, as the aim of the research was not to compare single AAL solutions to the respective counterparts of current practice in terms of effectiveness, future and more specific research is needed to answer the question of observability in detail. However, the results section presents the various facets of AAL, thereby emphasizing its potentials and therefore its positive attributes. In terms of **relative advantage** (whether it is better than current practice), AAL can be regarded as successful, assuming that technical and design challenges are appropriately dealt with in the development of the solutions. AAL can be regarded as being better than current practice, simply because it serves purposes that have not been addressed before, such as support with activities of daily living through technological means or the identification of gait-related problems through camera technologies, as shown by the results section (Amoretti, et al., 2011; Ayala, et al., 2012; Botia, et al., 2012; Chaaraoui, et al., 2012; Picking, et al., 2009; Pogorelc, Bosnic, et al., 2012). However, since the interaction with human caregivers is considerably reduced, it remains questionable if elderly people enjoy the same quality of caring when they are involved in AAL, which is to be answered by the actual application of AAL on a large scale and by future research (Botia, et al., 2012; Cardinaux, et al., 2011; Picking, et al., 2009; Pogorelc, Vatavu, et al., 2012). **Compatibility** presents the most severe challenging issue regarding AAL in the light of DoI, referring to values and perceptions of the target group towards the innovation. As shown by the results section, perceptions of the elderly towards AAL are not only positive (Belbachir, et al., 2010; Francioso, et al., 2011; Leone, et al., 2011; Meschner, et al., 2011). Quite the contrary, as data protection and privacy issues accompanied by a low technological knowledge hamper the positive perception of AAL (Ayala, et al., 2012; Cardinaux, et al., 2011). The reason for this may be, that today's generation of elderly people has not been growing up with technology and trust in technology in the same way as the coming generation does (Boulos, et al., 2007; Picking, et al., 2009). Moreover, as compatibility also refers to specific needs, elderly people may not necessarily see the need in AAL solutions, especially when they have to sacrifice their privacy and fear the exposure of their data. However, this is hypothesized and needs to be verified by future research. In terms of **trialability** – whether it is possible to try out the innovation – too less user involvement was identified by the results of this research (Ayala, et al., 2012; Belbachir, et al., 2010; Meschner, et al., 2011; O'Grady, et al., 2010; Pogorelc, Vatavu, et al., 2012; Weimar, et al., 2009). Moreover, as shown in the results section, AAL is hardly applied on a large scale (Belbachir, et al., 2010; Botia, et al., 2012; Cardinaux, et al., 2011; Meschner, et al., 2011; O'Grady, et al., 2010). Therefore, too less people of the target group are aware of it and thus cannot spread the word and make more people aware of its potential benefits. Referring to **complexity**, i.e. the simplicity of the innovation in terms of easy usage, AAL can be judged as meeting this characteristic in an adequate way. This is because AAL applications aim to ensure proactivity, in terms of the reduction of human interaction with the technology used (Ayala, et al., 2012; Botia, et al., 2012; Cardinaux, et al., 2011; O'Grady, et al., 2010; Picking, et al., 2009; Weimar, et al., 2009). However, when it comes to the interplay of solutions, i.e. the application of more than one AAL solution in a given environment, simplicity may be threatened as current AAL solutions are not aimed at working together yet, as identified by the results of this research (Amoretti, et al., 2011; Ayala, et al., 2012; Benghazi, et al., 2012; Chaaraoui, et al., 2012; Parente, et al., 2011; Rogers, et al., 2010). With a focus on **re-invention**, AAL has a high potential with regard to the possibility of altering and amending the innovation during implementation. Assuming that the interplay of solutions is ensured, which links to extendibility and integrability characteristics of single solutions, it is possible to 're-invent' AAL solutions and amend them according to changing needs of the elderly (Amoretti, et al., 2011; Benghazi, et al., 2012; Botia, et al., 2012; Cardinaux, et al., 2011; Parente, et al., 2011) .

5.2 Discussion of methods

In the next two paragraphs, advantages and disadvantages of the methodology are discussed. First, general advantages and disadvantages of the methods are mentioned, before advantages and limitations of the particular research are presented. With regard to the method 'document analysis', the Swiss Federal Institute of Technology Zurich identified certain attributes of a document analysis (2009). Accordingly, the biggest advantage of a document analysis is that it is not depending on the involvement of persons to answer specific questions. Moreover, it gives the possibility to gather material that is not included in observations or questionnaires. Additionally, monetary costs for a document analysis are low. However, the downsides of a document analysis are that it first demands much time to gather documents and especially to read the documents. Second, it may happen that documents on a specific issue or aspects are unavailable, missing, or not up to date. Moreover, a document analysis does not allow to measure opinions or needs. In terms of the EU actions towards AAL, seven specific fields of action were identified. In order to ensure a reliable presentation of the EU actions towards AAL, an amount of 22 documents was used for these seven fields. Hence, not only documents on specific strategies or initiatives were included, but also staff working documents on their progress, evaluations of outcomes, accompanying proposals and press releases. A limitation of the research on EU actions towards AAL is that it was difficult to determine if every kind of related documents was gathered and used. However, this was due to the complexity of the matched results on the website of the European Commission. Although certain limitation criteria can be ticked in the advanced search options, the search still resulted in a variety of documents that are not related to the field of interest. Moreover, sometimes documents were either not existing or unavailable, as for instance the evaluation of the sixth framework programme.

The second method that is used for this research is that of a systematic literature review, which also has certain advantages and disadvantages. According to the University of Brighton (2006), systematic reviews are a more objective assessment of literature on a certain topic compared with traditional reviews. Moreover, through the systematic nature, mistakes are prevented and the results give a valid presentation of a certain topic in a specified context and setting. Additionally, through the systematic manner, great amounts of information can be assessed and evaluated. Disadvantages of systematic reviews are that mostly little interest is spend on the actual competency of authors. Moreover, heterogeneity of the articles that a review results in is often not acknowledged. With regard to the systematic literature review on AAL, the inclusion of five databases with specific limitation criteria ensured a reliable presentation of research evidence of the chosen timeframe. The 22 articles that were gathered gave sufficient evidence and research findings to develop a categorization scheme of AAL by means of normalizing data. Furthermore, the 40 solutions discussed and mentioned in the articles were categorized in a mutually exclusive way. Therefore, the categorization can be regarded as strong and may even be used for future research, as no common and universally accepted categorization scheme exists so far. As also frequencies of emergence of solutions were recorded, it becomes evident what research focuses on the most, giving implications for future research. Moreover, challenges that exist with regard to AAL, were identified, grouped and allocated into different categories, too. By these means, a discussion of AAL on characteristics of a successful innovation was enabled. In terms of limitations of the research, a considerable limitation of the methodology is that it only focuses on AAL, without the inclusion of terms that go into the same direction as AAL, as for instance smart home applications. However, this can also be looked upon as an advantage, as the term ambient assisted living has only marginally spread over the borders of Europe. Thereby it was ensured that the research is absolutely European-focused. For the sake of simplicity and because people in public health do not necessarily hold deep technological knowledge that focuses on the interplay of hardware and software components, analysis within the systematic literature review focused on an understandable presentation of the results. Fall detection systems for instance, could have been split up in sensor-based and camera-based system, which however does not change the purpose of these kinds of systems.

5.3 Answer to the research question

At this point, answer to the research question 'What is the EU added value to ambient assisted living and what are challenges of diffusion of these innovative technologies' is provided. With regard to the EU added value to AAL, the results section 'EU actions towards AAL' has shown the progress of the EU with regard to ICT-enabled solutions for the elderly and AAL in particular. It can be stated that an added value is clearly visible, as the EU did a considerable amount of work in this field. Especially with the AAL Joint Programme initiated through the Action Plan on Ageing Well in the Information Society, the EU has made a big step in preparing for the implications of the demographic change by means of AAL. Furthermore, the EU has also acknowledged the benefits and feasibility of AAL solutions, as presented in the Action Plan of 2007. Moreover, with the allocation of large amounts of money, alone €600M into the AAL JP, the EU aims at boosting research into the direction of AAL. Additionally, the EU has taken measures to raise awareness on AAL, through ministerial conferences and online presence. However, there is a limitation of the EU's work, too, and therefore to the added value. This is, that actions towards ICT-enabled solutions for the elderly or AAL are sometimes either stated very general, or are not fulfilled in the way they were announced to be. An example for this is the announcement of an internet portal on ICT for the elderly within the Action Plan of 2007. Although an internet portal on ICT exists, it is kept very general and not targeted at the elderly population.

In terms of challenges for diffusion, the systematic literature review part of the results section and the discussion of AAL identified which challenges remain for AAL to be successfully deployed and used for the elderly population. One can assume that challenges on technological issues and design considerations will be eradicated if enough research and innovative thinking is carried out in coming research. Therefore, these two fields are not regarded as considerable challenges for the diffusion of AAL. However, as shown by the results section, a severe challenge that remains is that of acceptance from the side of the elderly, i.e. the target group. As long as the elderly population perceive AAL as cutting into their privacy and fear that their data is not protected appropriately, the diffusion is hampered. Moreover, AAL is hardly applied on a large scale with involvement of elderly, as identified by the research evidence. Thereby, the innovation of AAL cannot be communicated through the inter-personal channels, which the theory of Rogers identified as a strong instrument for the quality and pace of the adoption process. In sum, challenges that remain for the diffusion of AAL exist in compatibility and trialability of which acceptance challenges in the light of compatibility weigh the heaviest.

5.4 Recommendations and conclusion

In order to ensure the successful diffusion of AAL, research of this study has led to the following recommendations for future research and the general dealing with AAL:

> Research should aim at decreasing or eliminating technological challenges and challenges in the design of AAL. Especially important is the application of AAL on a large scale in order to identify challenges and requirements that lab-environments and low-scale applications cannot reveal. Moreover, fall detection has been researched enormously; therefore other domains should be at the focus of future research, as for instance support with activities of daily living.

> The target group of AAL, i.e. the elderly population, should be involved in future research in order to ensure that needs and wishes are addressed appropriately. Moreover, these measures should ensure that elderly people develop positive attitudes towards AAL in order to enhance diffusion, as inter-personal communication channels are identified as having a severe impact on the quality and pace of diffusion.

> Future research on AAL should focus on the interplay of solutions in order to ensure that AAL solutions can easily be put together to fulfill the specific needs and wishes that an individual elderly may have.

> Future research should focus on developing core-technologies for ambient assisted living solutions. These core-technologies should preferably be the underlying technology for all future solutions, as this would make extendibility to other solutions

and the amendment of solutions to changing needs over time much easier. Although the AAL JP already has a common evaluation procedure for projects, this should be extended to the requirement of these core-technologies, which would further simplify the application.

Diffusion of AAL can only be enhanced and ensured, when AAL is communicated not only to health care professionals, policy makers and programmers, but also to people of the general population, regardless whether they are in need for AAL solutions or not. Thereby awareness on AAL can easily be raised.

The research evidence of this study led to the conclusion, that AAL may not be suitable for today's generation of elderly people, due to severe challenges in acceptance from sides of the target group. However, as the implications of the demographic change today are not as severe as they will be in 30 years, this does not necessarily present a problem. Yet, a total replacement of humans with technology may be a step too big at the moment, as it may hamper or even interrupt the diffusion of AAL in general. This scenario could ultimately result in a too less proceeded diffusion process at the time when AAL is desperately needed.

References

AAL Joint Programme. (2008). *Programme information – Brochure*. Retrieved 15.05.2012 from: http://www.aal-europe.eu/Published/pr-docs/aalflyerv2

AAL Joint Programme. (2012). *Call for Proposals 2012*. Retrieved 15.05.2012 from: http://www.aal-europe.eu/calls/call-5-2012/Call5_v4_20120326_final.pdf

Amoretti, M., Copelli, S., Wientapper, F., Furfari, F., Lenzi, S., & Chessa, S. (2011). Sensor data fusion for activity monitoring in the PERSONA ambient assited living project. *Ambient Intell Human Comput*. doi: 10.1007/s12652-011-0095-6

Ayala, I., Amor, M., & Fuentes, L. (2012). Self-configuring agents for ambient assisted living applications. *Pers Ubiquit Comput*. doi: 10.1007/s00779-012-0555-9

Belbachir, A. N., Drobics, M., & Marschitz, W. (2010). Ambient Assisted Living for ageing well – an overview. *Elektrotechnik & Informationstechnik, 127*(7-8), 6. doi: 10.1007/s00502-010-0747-9

Benghazi, K., Hurtado, M. V., Hornos, M. J., Rodríguez, M. L., Rodríguez-Domínguez, C., Pelegrina, A. B., & Rodríguez-Fórtiz, M. J. (2012). Enabling correct design and formal analysis of Ambient Assisted Living systems. *The Journal of Systems and Software, 85*, 498-510. doi: 10.1016/j.jss.2011.05.022

Botia, J. A., Villa, A., & Palma, J. (2012). Ambient Assisted Living systems for in-home monitoring of healthy independent elders. *Expert Systems with Applications, 39*, 8136-8148. doi: 10.1016/j.eswa.2012.01.153

Boulos, M. N. K., Rocha, A., Martins, A., Vicente, M. E., Bolz, A., Feld, R., Tchoudovski, I., Braecklein, M., Nelson, J., Ó Laighin, G., Sdogati, C., Cesaroni, F., Antomarini, M., Jobes, A.& Kinirons, M. (2007). CAALYX: A new generation of location-based services in healthcare. *International Journal of Health Geographics, 6*(9). doi: 10.1186/1476-072X-6-9

Cardinaux, F., Bhowmik, D., Abhayartne, C., & Hawley, M. S. (2011). Video based technology for ambient assisted living: A review of the literature. *Journal of Ambient Intelligence and Smart Environment, 3*, 253-269. doi: 10.3233/AIS-2011-0110

Chaaraoui, A. A., Climent-Pérez, P., & Flórez-Revuelta, F. (2012). A review on vision techniques applied to Human Behaviour Analysis for Ambient-Assisted Living. *Expert Systems with Applications, 39*, 10873-10888. doi: 10.1016/j.eswa.2012.03.005

Clarke, R. (1999). A Primer in Diffusion of Innovations Theory Retrieved 29.01.2012, from http://www.rogerclarke.com/SOS/InnDiff.html

Commission of the European Communities. (2002). *Council decision of 30 September 2002 adopting a specific programme for research, technological development and demonstration: 'Integrating and strengthening the European Research Area' (2002 to 2006). (2002/834/EC)*. Luxembourg: Official Journal of the European Communities.

Commission of the European Communities. (2007a). Communication from the Commission to the European Parliament, the Council, the European Economic and Social Committee and the Committee of the Regions. *Ageing well in the Information Society. Action Plan on Information and Communication Technologies and Ageing*. Retrieved 30.04.2012 from:

http://eur-lex.europa.eu/LexUriServ/site/en/com/2007/com2007_0332en01.pdf

Commission of the European Communities. (2007b). Communication from the Commission to the European Parliament, the Council, the European Economic and Social Committee and the Committee of the Regions. *European i2010 initiative on e-Inclusion*. Retrieved 30.04.2012 from:

http://ec.europa.eu/information_society/activities/einclusion/docs/i2010_initiative/com_native_com_2007_0694_f_en_acte.pdf

Commission of the European Communities. (2009a). Europe's Digital Competitiveness Report – Main achievments of the i2010 strategy 2005-2009. Staff Working Document. Retrieved 30.04.2012 from:

http://ec.europa.eu/information_society/eeurope/i2010/docs/annual_report/2009/sec_009_1060.pdf

Commission of the European Communities. (2009b). Communication from the European Parliament, the European Economic and Social Committee and the Committee of the Regions on the progress made under the Seventh European Framework Programme for Research. Retrieved 27.05.2012 from:

http://eurlex.europa.eu/LexUriServ/LexUriServ.do?uri=COM:2009:0209:FIN:EN:PD

European Commission. (2002a). *The sixth framework programme (2002-2006): Decision no2002/1513/EC of the European Parliament and of the council : concerning the sixth framework programme of the European Community for research, technologicaldevelopment and demonstration activities, contributing to the creation of theEuropean Research Area and to innovation (2002-2006)*. Luxembourg: Office forOfficial Publications of the European Communities.

European Commission. (2002b). The Sixth Framework Programme in brief. Retrieved 22.03.2012, from: http://ec.europa.eu/research/fp6/pdf/fp6-in-brief_en.pdf

European Commission. (2005). Commission launches five-year strategy to boost the digital economy [Press release IP/05/643]. Retrieved 30.4.2012 from: http://europa.eu/rapid/pressReleasesAction.do?reference=IP/07/831&format=HTML aged=0&language=EN&guiLanguage=en

European Commission. (2006a). *The seventh framework programme (2007-2013): Decision No 1982/2006/EC of the European Parliament and of the Council concerning the Seventh Framework Programme of the European Community for research, technological development and demonstration activities (2007-2013)*. Luxembourg: Office for Official Publications of the European Communities.

European Commission. (2006b). *Decision 2006/971/EC of the Council concerning the Specific Programme "Cooperation" implementing the Seventh Framework Programme of the European Community for research, technological development anddemonstration activities (2007 to 2013)*. Luxembourg: Office for Official Publications of the European Communities.

European Commission. (2006). Riga Ministerial Declaration. Retrieved 30.04.2012 from: http://ec.europa.eu/information_society/events/ict_riga_2006/doc/declaration_riga.pdf

European Commission. (2007a). European e-Inclusion Initiative. *First Contributions to the Campaign "e-Inclusion: be part of it!"*. Retrieved 30.04.2012 from: http://ec.europa.eu/information_society/activities/einclusion/docs/bepartofit/contribut ons_booklet.pdf

European Commission. (2007b). Ministerial Debate on European e-Inclusion Policy. Retrieved 14.05.2012 from: http://ec.europa.eu/information_society/events/einclusion_lisbon/programme/index_e .htm

European Commission. (2007c). €1bn in digital technologies for Europeans to age well [Press Release IP/07/831]. Retrieved 14.05.1989 from: http://europa.eu/rapid/pressReleasesAction.do?reference=IP/07/831&format=HTML aged=0&language=EN&guiLanguage=en

European Commission. (2007d). Preparation of the Competiveness Council of Ministers, Brussels, 28 September 2007. Retrieved 15.05.2012 from: http://europa.eu/rapid/pressReleasesAction.do?reference=MEMO/07/384&format= ML&aged=0&language=EN

European Commission. (2008a). *Seniorwatch 2 – Assessment of the Senior Markt for ICT Progress and Developments*. Final Report. Retrieved 14.05.2012 from:
http://ec.europa.eu/information_society/activities/einclusion/docs/swa2finalreport.pdf

European Commission. (2008b). *The Ambient Assisted Living (AAL) Joint Programme* Retrieved 15.05.2012 from:
http://ec.europa.eu/information_society/activities/einclusion/docs/rtd_docs/aal_overview_16_june_2008.pdf

European Commission. (2010a). Communication from the Commission. Europe 2020. *A strategy for smart, sustainable and inclusive growth*. Retrieved 30.04.2012 from:
http://eurlex.europa.eu/LexUriServ/LexUriServ.do?uri=COM:2010:2020:FIN:EN:PF

European Commission. (2010b). Communication from the Commission to the European Parliament, the Council, the European Economic and Social Committee and the Committee of the Regions. *A Digital Agenda for Europe*. Retrieved 30.04.2012 from:
http://ec.europa.eu/information_society/digital-agenda/documents/digital-agenda communication-en.pdf

European Parliament. (2012). Parliamentary question 27 April 2012. E-004427/2012. Retrieved 15.05.2012 from:
http://www.europarl.europa.eu/sides/getDoc.do?secondRef=0&language=EN&type WQ&reference=E-2012-004427

Eurostat. (2012a). Fertility Statistics. Retrieved 15.03.2012, from
http://epp.eurostat.ec.europa.eu/statistics_explained/index.php/Fertility_statistics

Eurostat. (2012b). Total fertility rate, 1960-2009 (live births per woman). Retrieved 15.03.2012 from:
http://epp.eurostat.ec.europa.eu/statistics_explained/index.php/Fertility_statistics

Francioso, L., Pascali, C. D., Farella, I., Martucci, C., Creti, P., Siciliano, P., & Perrone, A. (2011). Flexible thermoelectric generator for ambient assisted living wearable biometric sensors. *Journal of Power Sources, 196*, 3239-32433. doi: 10.1016/j.jpowsour.2010.11.081

Golafshani, N. (2003). Understanding Reliability and Validity in Qualitative Research. *The Qualitative Report, 8*(4), 597 - 607.

Grundy, E., Tomassini, C., & Festy, P. (2006). Demographic change and the care of older people: introduction. *Eur J Population, 22*, 215-218. doi: 10.1007/s10680-006-9005-6

Jara, A. J., Zamora, M. A., & Skarmeta, A. F. G. (2009). An Architecture for Ambient Assisted Living and Health Environments *IWANN 2009, Part II, LNCS 5518* (pp. 882-889): Springer-Verlag Berlin Heidelberg.

Kaminski, J. (2011). Diffusion of Innovation Theory. *Canadian Journal of Nursing Informatics, 6*(2).

Lee, R. D., & Reher, D. S. (2011). The Landscape of Demographic Transition and its Aftermath. *Population and Development Review, 37*, 1-7.

Leone, A., Diraco, G., & Siciliano, P. (2011). Detecting falls with 3D range camera in ambient assisted living applications: A preliminary study. *Medical Engineering & Physics, 33*(770-781). doi: 10.1016/j.medengphy.2011.02.001

Lutz, W. (2006). Fertility rates and future population trends: Will Europe's birth rate recover or continue to decline? *International Journal of Andrology, 29*, 25-33.

Market Street Research. (n.d.). *Workbook B - Conducting Secondary Research*. Retrieved 16.01.2012 from: http://www.marketstreetresearch.com/wallace/Workbook%20B%20%20Secondary%20research.pdf

Meschner, P., Prinz, A., Koene, P., Köbler, F., Altmann, M., Krcmar, H., & Leimeister, J. M. (2011). Reaching into patients' homes - participatory designed AAL services. *Electron Markets, 21*, 63-76. doi: 10.1007/s12525-011-0050-6

Moumtzi, V., Wills, C., & Koumpis, A. (2010). Service composition to support ambient assisted living solutions for the elderly. Thessaloniki, Greece, London, UK: ALTEC Software S.A./Research Programmes Division

Kingston University/Faculty of Computing, Information Systems & Mathematics.

Munoz, A., Augusto, J. C., Villa, A., & Botia, J. A. (2011). Design and evaluation of an ambient assisted living system based on an argumentative multi-agent system. *Pers Ubiquit Comput, 15*, 377-387. doi: 10.1007/s00779-010-0361-1

Neuman, W. L. (2006). *Social research methods: Qualitative and quantitative approaches*. Boston, Massachusetts

O'Grady, M. J., Muldoon, C., Dragone, M., Tynan, R., & O'Hare, G. M. P. (2010). Towards evolutionary ambient assisted living systems. *Ambient Intell Human Comput, 1*, 15-29. doi: 10.1007/s12652-009-0003-5

Official Journal of the European Union. (2008). *Decision No 742/2008/EC of the European Parliament and of the Council on the Community's participation in a research and development programme undertaken by several Member States aimed at enhancingthe quality of life of older people through the use of new information and communication technologies.* L 201/49. Retrieved 15.05.2012 from:ftp://ftp.cordis.europa.eu/pub/fp7/art169/docs/aal.pdf

Orr, G. (2003). Diffusion of Innovations Retrieved 29.01.2012, from http://www.stanford.edu/class/symbsys205/Diffusion%20of%20Innovations.htm

Parente, G., Nugent, C. C., Hong, X., Donnelly, M. P., Chen, L., & Vicario, E. (2011). Formal Modeling Techniques for Ambient Assisted Living. *Ageing Int, 36*, 192-216. doi: 10.1007/s12126-010-9086-8

Picking, R., Robinet, A., Grout, V., McGinn, J., Roy, A., Ellis, S., & Oram, D. (2009). A Case Study Using a Methodological Approach to Developing User Interfaces for Elderly and Disabled People. *The Computer Journal, 53*(6). doi: 10.1093/comjnl/bxp089

Pogorelc, B., Bosnic, Z., & Gams, M. (2012). Automatic recognition of gait-related health problems in the elderly using machine learning. *Multimed Tools Appl, 58*, 333-354. doi: 10.1007/s11042-011-0786-1

Pogorelc, B., Vatavu, R., Lugmayr, A., Stockleben, B., Risse, T., Kaario, J., Lomonaco, E. C. & Gams, M. (2012). Semantic ambient media: From ambient advertising to ambient-assisted living. *Multimed Tools Appl, 58*, 399-425. doi: 10.1007/s11042-011-0917-8

Pope, C., Ziebland, S., & Mays, N. (2000). Analysing qualitative data. In C. Pope & N. Mays (Eds.), *Qualitative Research in Health Care* (2nd ed., pp. 114-116): BMJ Books.

Robinson, L. (2009). *A summary of Diffusion of Innovations.* Retrieved 10.07.2012 from: http://www.enablingchange.com.au/Summary_Diffusion_Theory.pdf

Rodrigues, G. N., Alves, V., Silveira, R., & Laranjeira, L. A. (2012). Dependability analysis in the Ambient Assisted Living Domain: An explenatory case study. *The Journal of Systems and Software, 85*, 112-131. doi: 10.1016.j.ss.2011.07.037

Rogers, E. M. (2003). *Diffusion of Innovations* (5th ed.). New York: Free Press.

Rogers, E. M. & Scott, K. L. (1997). *The Diffusion of Innovations Model and Outreach from the National Network of Libraries of Medicine to Native American Communities.* Retrieved 10.07.2012 from: http://nnlm.gov/archive/pnr/eval/rogers.html

Rogers, R., Peres, Y., & Mueller, W. (2010). Living longer independently – a healthcare interoperability perspective. *Elektrotechnik & Informationstechnik, 7*(8), 6. doi: 10.1007/s00502-010-0748-8

Ruyter, B. d., Zwartkruis-Pelgrim, E., & Aarts, E. (2010). Ambient Assisted Living Research in the CareLab. *GeroPsych, 23*(2).

Srp, Á., & Vajda, F. (2010). Possible techniques and issues in fall detection using asynchronous temporalcontrast sensors. *Elektrotechnik & Informationstechnik, 127*(7-8), 7. doi: 10.1007/s00502-010-0751-0

Swiss Federal Institute of Technology Zurich. (2009). *General information about document analysis*. Retrieved 01.07.2012 from: http://www.evalguide.ethz.ch/eval_general/methods_of_evaluation/document_analys_EN

University of Brighton. (2006). *Evidence-based practice tutorial: Systematic Reviews – a brief overview*. Retrieved 01.07.2012 from: http://www.brighton.ac.uk/ncor/tutorials/EBP_Tutorial_Systematic_reviews_overvie.pdf

Villacorta, J. J., Val, L. d., Jimanez, M. I., & Izquierdo, A. (2010). Security System Technologies Applied to Ambient Assisted Living. Valladolid, Spain: E.T.S.I. Telecomunicación, Universidad de Valladolid.

Weimar, U., Simpson, R., Barsan, N., Heine, T., Simmendinger, W., Malfatti, M., Margesin, B., Gonzo, L., Grassid, M., Lombardi, A., Malcovati, P., Leone, A., Diraco, G., Siciliano, P., Sicard, O. v., Pohle, R., Fleischer, M., Redaelli, A., Giacosi, A. & Bonassi, C. (2009). Microsystem Technology for Ambient Assisted Living (AAL). *Procedia Chemistry, 1*, 710-713. doi: 10.1016/j.proche.2009.07.177